Learning to Talk

A PARENTS' GUIDE FOR THE FIRST FIVE YEARS

MARGARET C. L. GREENE

ILLUSTRATIONS BY JILL HASSELL

HARPER & BROTHERS · NEW YORK

LEARNING TO TALK

Copyright © 1960 by M. C. L. Greene

Printed in the United States of America

FIRST EDITION

B-K

Grateful acknowledgment is made for permission to quote brief selections from the following:

"Learning to Talk" from Collected Poems of C. Day Lewis: Jonathan Cape, Ltd.

"Earth's Treasure" from All Different by Ruth Ainsworth: William Heinemann, Ltd.

"I Keep Six Honest Serving Men" from Just So Stories by Rudyard Kipling: Mrs. George Bambridge, Messrs. Macmillan, A. P. Watt & Son, and Doubleday & Company, Inc.

"Nanny" from She Shanties by A. P. Herbert: Sir A. P. Herbert, A. P. Watt & Son, Ernest Benn, Ltd., the Proprietors of Punch, and Doubleday & Company, Inc.

Library of Congress catalog card number: 60-7541

LEARNING TO TALK

To my daughters

Contents

Learning to Talk

Tongue trips, recovers, triumphs,
Turning all ways to express
What the forward eye can guess—
That time is his and earth young.
                C. Day Lewis

Foreword

This is a delightful little book, full of good sense and accurate information about how babies become human beings through the acquisition of speech. All parents should find it readable, helpful, and interesting. It is an original work of considerable flavor. Parents need this information, and they enjoy such books, especially when they are written with the warmth Mrs. Greene shows.

Practicing speech therapists should find it useful to lend to parents of their very young cases, and pediatricians too should find it valuable.

The book reads easily. Its transitions are good, and its sentence structure is varied. The author talks to the reader and you sense her personal charm. She writes cleanly, without academic or professional cant. Her quotations and illustrative anecdotes are pointed and vivid, and she has the ability to turn a phrase so that it has focus.

Learning to Talk is accurate in its information. The author's statements on child rearing—and this book is as much a book on how to raise a child as it is on how to teach him to talk—are sensible and supported by the best thought in modern child psychology.

In view of the growing interest in children's speech and its development and the attractiveness of this little book, I predict its wide use.

> CHARLES VAN RIPER
> Professor of Speech and Director
> of Speech and Hearing Clinic,
> Western Michigan University

An Introduction for Parents

Why do adults find it so difficult to learn a foreign language when children learn to speak with no apparent difficulty? This is a question I am often asked. It is of course easier for a toddler to learn his mother tongue than for a grownup to learn another language. For one thing, a toddler learns the play way and has nothing much else to do all day. He also has an absorbing interest in speech which gives him an incentive to talk and a readiness to learn, which is unsurpassed at any other stage of human development. Moreover, he has only one language to listen to and what he hears falls on fallow ground. He has no preconceived ideas about language. An adult, in learning to speak a foreign tongue, has to lay aside what he knows of his own. He has to discard the words he knows and learn others and so he is constantly in the predicament of having to translate before he speaks. Familiar and deeply ingrained habits concerning the word order of sentences have to be overcome and words rearranged according to quite different language rules. Not least, one has to try to get rid of one's native intonation and stress, and the melody of one's mother tongue, and to learn a quite different tune. This is perhaps the most difficult thing of all for us to do when learning another language.

From many points of view, therefore, it *is* easier for a tiny child than for an adult to learn to speak a language. But is it really as easy for a child to learn to talk as it appears to be at first sight? No. In actual fact it is not so very easy. It takes a child a good five years to learn pronunciation and enough language to be able to express himself at all adequately, and he goes on learning and perfecting the skill for many more years than this. During the first five years of his life the child is listening attentively to adult speech, attempting to imitate what he hears and reproduce it, practicing words and then sentences, step by step, day after day, year after year. Of all the skills the child masters during the pre-school years, learning to talk is by far the most difficult and most marvelous. This great achievement is only accomplished through his parents and more especially his mother teaching him all these hours, days and years. Unlike learning to sit, to crawl and to walk, which baby will do when he has sufficient motor control of his body and with very little if any outside help, baby will not learn to talk without much patient teaching from the adults who surround him.

Fortunately most parents give their children exactly the right sort of help at the right time, intuitively attuning their speech to suit a child's immature understanding. Mothers, on the whole, are so good at this that neither they nor their babies realize what is happening—that mother is teacher and baby the pupil. All the speech hurdles that crop up are taken in their stride and the average child born "with no language but a cry" eventually learns to speak perfectly and without anybody's being aware that there was any difficulty. This is how it should be. But not all babies are fortunate in having mothers who are expert in mothercraft without ever having had any special instruction. Perhaps these lucky and gifted "motherly" women remember their own childhood and mothers better than others can, or perhaps they were just fortunate in having mothers who were "instinct" with mothercraft. Be this as it may, some parents have little intuition to guide them in bringing up their babies, and little insight either into the stages in speech development which children normally pass through. So they may miss opportunities of giving help when it is needed, or try to give help when it is not needed, and this may actually hold up the chances of a little mite's learning to talk. Certainly without much insight into how a baby learns to talk you will miss much of the joy and delight that come from listening to your child's prattle. Listening to his mistakes as he embarks upon more and more difficult linguistic exploits and knowing what he is about will teach you a real admiration for this most wonderful of human achievements—of just learning to talk.

Yes, listening to your little girl or boy talking is undoubtedly the most delightful entertainment and the most adorable aspect of his growing up to be five. Without knowing what your baby is doing and why, when he says "gog" for "dog" or "genkum" for "gentleman," invents words and even his own language, jumbles sentences higgledy-piggledy, calls the repair man "Daddy" and a jet a "birdie," you miss a lot. Worse still, you may even become anxious at these normal growing pains in your youngster's speech, become so critical and dissatisfied over his performance that you embark upon a program of speech correction. But Heaven forbid that you should! This will at best destroy your enjoyment and that of your child in his fascinating performance, and at worst actively delay his learning to talk properly. This is a real danger. And it is with the sincere hope that I can add something to some parents' enjoyment of their babies' talking and help others to avoid mistakes in teaching, that this book is written.

Before I write further I must make an important point clear. Although I shall mention constantly the ages at which babies reach certain stages or milestones in speech development, these are purely a matter of convenience to provide signposts, as it were, on our pathway through the five important years of development with which we are concerned. The ages given are those for the average child, but actually there is no such thing as an average child because one child is quite different from another. No two children even in the same family, with the same environment and parents, develop alike. One child walks at a year, the next at eighteen months or two years. There is a very great range in maturation rate or speed of development in all spheres: in sitting, crawling, walking and especially in talking. Also, little girls are generally earlier in all stages of talking than little boys. Many perfectly normal babies do not fulfill the expectations of the average child and may be six months late in babbling and nine months to a year in saying the first words, and yet develop perfectly normal speech by the age of four or five. "Average" therefore allows a great deal of latitude and there is no need to worry if your baby does not follow the textbooks exactly.

The main thing to grasp in this study of speech development is the *sequence* of events: that a baby coos before he babbles, and understands words before he speaks any, and says single words before he says sentences. It is no use expecting him to skip a vital stage; for instance, he cannot say words before he babbles any more than he can crawl before he sits. This is only common sense, you will say—but plenty of parents, though appreciating this principle with regard to babies' motor development, for some reason or other take a quite different view when it comes to babies' talking. In their ignorance of the normal developmental stages of speaking some parents may apply quite different standards or try to force the child's pace, to exact perfect pronunciation, for example, long before a child is capable of producing it.

Throughout I will try to illustrate my points with actual examples of children's speech which I have collected from my own daughters and the children of friends, and I also include some of the famous examples recorded in literature which are too charming to be omitted. There are of course many wonderfully detailed and careful studies of children's speech to be read by those who wish to study the subject further. For these parents a small reading list is given at the end of this book. This book itself is only intended as a simple introduction to beginners in parenthood.

MARGARET C. L. GREENE

LEARNING TO TALK

I
The First Twelve Months

For all earth's treasure round me lies,
And I have ears and hands and eyes.

Ruth Ainsworth

How soon should one start thinking about this important matter of teaching one's baby to talk? When should one set about helping him? The answer is the moment he is born. Of course he cannot understand what you say for a long time but he very soon grows to like you talking to him. At first he may not take much notice, it is true, and the only noises he seems to hear are loud ones which startle him and make him jump and then cry. However, in an extraordinarily short time he begins to take notice of mother's voice and footsteps as she approaches his crib. At three or four weeks you will find you can soothe him momentarily if he is crying just by crooning to him sympathetically. He is also upset very early by an angry voice. If you can catch his eye at four to six weeks (it probably *is* only an eye at this stage since he can focus with only one eye at a time and often squints most horribly as a result) and talk to him, telling him what a beautiful clever little one he is, he may actually smile back. Now don't let father spoil it and don't believe him when he declares it only "wind." It may be, but on the other hand it probably is a real, genuine, heart-warming smile, your baby's first real social response and therefore very, very important. You have made contact with him, he loves you and returns your love for him.

Your baby's first smile is perhaps one of the most beautiful and satisfying experiences of motherhood—at least it was for me. What is more, it is a landmark in social relations. Some abnormal children never respond to speech in this way, acknowledging mother is there, glowing in the warmth of her love and tenderness. Such children, not very surprisingly, develop very oddly indeed, and may even become schizophrenics. We do not know whether these babies are cold and aloof to begin with, or whether they become like this because their mothers have not enveloped them in an atmosphere of love and security. At least we do know for certain that a warm and loving atmosphere is an absolutely essential ingredient to a baby's healthy emotional development. So take no chances; look out for baby's first smile and encourage him with the love talk he already understands.

Besides these early indications that baby is interested in your talking to him, there are interesting developments in the progress he is making in vocalizing on his own account. To begin with baby only cries to exercise his lungs and voice, as a result of internal promptings such as tummy-ache or hunger. Very soon, however, the discerning parents can distinguish between different gradations of crying: the loud harsh hunger cry, the cry of pain, the complaining cry of loneliness or perhaps boredom. At first the baby is just producing an automatic primitive reaction to discomfort with no intention of telling anybody anything, but when mother comes to tend to his needs day after day, he learns, in no time at all, to connect crying with her coming. She, in her turn, is interpreting those cries. So, in an important way, the first link in communication between the child and the mother is established. Crying brings results. The faint glimmerings of an awareness of the possibilities of noising his needs abroad are dawning and a seed is sown in his psychology which will grow apace.

After a month baby produces some other sounds besides those

of crying and inelegantly burping up wind after a feeding. He begins to make noises which are recognizably human. When fed and contented he starts cooing and gurgling, trilling up and down the scale—a joyous performance, a sure sign of baby's happiness and well-being, and real music to a mother's ears. Gradually the repertoire of the infant performer increases with little squeals and chirrups akin to laughter, with spluttering and blowing raspberries. A very forward baby as early as two months will reply with coos and squeals if you encourage him with smiling and talking. Incredible as it may seem he is already replying when addressed. Toward the end of the first month the baby is attentive to sounds and listens to music, trying to localize its source by eye. Now at three months he turns his head, especially when he hears a voice. At three months baby may even repeat a sound you make if it is one he has just been practicing himself. Eying the speaker, listening attentively and imitating are the first essentials in learning to talk, so play with your baby in this way sometimes after a feeding. Be careful not to overtax his attention though. His concentration is very short at this age and, though the game may be fun for you, baby tires very readily. If you persist in trying to hold his attention he may suddenly burst into disconcerting wails. He is letting you know he has had enough. This holds true too at six, eight and even nine months, incidentally.

Some parents tell me they would not dream of cooing or gurgling at their baby in the nonsensical way I recommend. But how lovely it is to see a mother cradling her baby in her arms and crooning to him, or to see a father tickling Johnnie's tummy and babbling, "Boo—boo—boo to you, young man," while Johnnie chortles and chuckles, "talking back." In such intimate scenes of loving sympathy and understanding, the child grows up with a sense of security and learns to delight in his own "talking," which brings such approval and enjoyment.

Many children who do not speak at all till three or four years are reported never to have cooed or babbled very much in the early months. I often wonder whether this was because the child could not or whether he was left too much on his own and not encouraged to vocalize. It is difficult to prove either way, I admit, but at least you can make sure that you give your baby plenty of stimulation. Take no risks by depriving him of opportunities to listen to you and encourage him to try out his own voice too.

Talk to your baby

I know of at least one little boy who suffered because his parents deliberately avoided talking to him for the first year. Anthony was born with a cleft palate, which is not as a rule repaired until a year old. His father and mother got the idea that if he babbled before the operation he would learn to talk through his nose. Well, the operation was successful and speech, when it came, was not in the least nasal, but he made no attempt to talk until two years old, and his speech remained very babyish until past five.

Young Anthony suffered from lack of help with speech in the first year.

At about three months old cooing makes way for more ambitious sounds and now baby begins to exercise his tongue and jaws and lips as well as his voice, and to utter syllables. This is the beginning of babbling, which is in full spate by four or five months. He starts with a simple "da," "ya," "ga" or "ba" interspersed with coos, but gradually long repetitive strings develop. You can hear baby practicing his speech exercises happily in his carriage or crib, kicking his legs and jerking his arms as he goes into a sort of mass action of which articulation is only one of many motor activities. This is the prelinguistic phase of speech development. It is as natural for the human child to babble as it is for a bird to sing a song, a dog to bark or a cock to crow. Babbling is the inherited raw material of speech handed down through the ages from generation to generation in the human race. The child babbles without having to be taught and without having to learn these sounds; they just pour from his lips and have no meaning. Nevertheless, they exercise tongue, lips and voice, and babbling is an essential forerunner to the mastery of pronunciation: the articulation of the vowels and consonants of real speech.

By four to five months baby should be playing with strings of the same syllable and experimenting with different combinations as well. His sounds are not so clear as those we use in adult speech because he has not got the necessary fine muscular control of his tongue, but syllables are recognizable as "da-da-da-," "gu-gu-gu-," "mum-mum-mum-," etc., and are already distinguishable one from another. Of course this increased skill coincides with an all-round improvement in performance. Baby no longer plays with his fingers, toes and feet, exploring his own body, but is attempting to sit and to grasp and handle toys. Now banging, bouncing and babbling all develop together in an active, lively youngster. Most important too is that he is now on solid foods and learning to chew and shift food around his mouth with his tongue.

Up to date I have stressed the aspect of the baby's vocabulary, the sounds he can be expected to make in the early months and how to encourage him to do this. But even more important is what you say to baby during this early stage, and not only this but every later stage. The wise mother talks to her little one all the time she is bathing, feeding, dressing and playing with him. Never imagine there is no need to talk to him because he doesn't understand. For many months he doesn't, it is quite true, but all the time he is absorbing the rhythm and inflection and the emotional content of your speech. He recognizes, for instance, a good-tempered or impatient tone very early. And though he does not understand individual words he understands the sort of talk appropriate to certain situations: the way mother talks when putting on his clothes or feeding him. He understands the total setup of which speech is an integral part; he understands what might be described as the linguistic situation. He is, in fact, observing, taking a part in operations and above all *listening*. The ability to listen is an essential part of the preparation for learning to speak. It forms the basis of imitating speech and therefore of speaking. A running commentary from his mother is just what baby needs to hear. The repetition of little sentences, putting names to things and to doing things are necessary auditory training.

Baby is most assuredly helped in listening if his mother modifies her speech to his infant intelligence, not talking as she would to an adult but as to a baby. There is no need to talk baby talk, but there is a real need to speak slowly, simply and repetitively, stressing key words, such as nouns and verbs (the words for things and doing things), and referring always to the present and familiar in baby's experience. A baby learns more easily from the following sample of motherly prattle than the more adult way in which one might address him.

"Now up you get. Off with your pajamas. Here's your vest. Over your head it goes. That's fine. Now your pants. Here they are. In go your feet. There's one. There's two. Here's your sweater.

Over your head now. Pull. Over it goes. Peekaboo! That's fine.
Now your socks. That's one. Now the other. That's two. And
now your shoes," etc.

You are teaching a lot of language through this sort of talk.
Soon the child is co-operating, stretching out arms and legs,
suiting the action to the words and clearly understanding. It is a
game too. Learning the play way.

Such a direct method of addressing your small offspring in
simple terms is far more effective than the policy of verbalizing
one's own thoughts to the child adult fashion, which amounts to
little more than talking to oneself as far as the child is concerned.

"Now then, it's time to get up. I've collected all your clothes
and got them ready here. Sit still and try not to fidget while I
dress you. It's already late and I must be quick with the breakfast or father will miss his train."

Maybe the play way takes longer but in the long run probably
not. I don't mind betting the first child will fidget less and start
the day a happier baby than the second. Also I am certain he will
be doing things for himself earlier and so helping you.

This early training in listening to speech is essential to learning
to speak. I cannot stress this fact too much. It is so important
that it is now recognized that deaf children need to be given a
hearing aid long before the age of one year, and as early as three
months if deafness can be diagnosed that early, and sometimes
it can be. The sooner a baby becomes familiar with the tunes of
speech and is trained to listen, the better it is. A severely deaf
child, if given a hearing aid before nine months, will speak earlier
and far better than a child no more deaf but not given an aid
till two or three. A child needs to grow up with speech ringing
in his ears from the day he is born and then he will learn to imitate these sounds more and more readily, until it is quite easy
for him at a year to say words spontaneously.

Although we get an inkling that baby is beginning to understand what we say to him at seven months, it is difficult to deter-

mine how much he understands from speech and how much from seeing what is going on around him. By eight months, however, it becomes obvious that he is really beginning to understand speech. Instead of showing excitement only when placed at the table and waiting for his dinner, he may show excitement at the mere mention of dinner. He will look at a toy or reach for it when it is named as a result of mother's repeatedly naming and showing it. He can obey little commands too, such as "Dance for Daddy" or "Wave bye-bye." You will find you can fool him at first by changing the consonants of these familiar phrases he has heard, as long as you retain the same vowels and exactly the same intonation or tune. You may say "Bate my-my," and he will wave bye-bye obediently, or "Glance for waggy" and dance he will! He is not really recognizing consonants yet but he learns fast and at nine or ten months he can no longer be tricked in this way. He needs the right formula and also a sensible formula to suit the occasion. For example, he will no longer wave good-bye when there is no question of leave-taking in the offing. Formerly he would perform his little tricks like an automaton at any time with no realization of the real meaning. Now he is obtaining some insight into all that is taking place around him. He also understands a great many more commands, for with the recognition of words comes real understanding of their meaning and of what is required of him.

Now, while your baby is advancing rapidly in understanding what is said to him, he is still not speaking himself. He is able to imitate far more easily the sounds made by his parents as long as these are in his babble vocabulary, and even if they are not he has a try. But he uses his own mastered syllables, not exactly those you say to him. Developing side by side with this skill is manual dexterity. At first baby could only grasp objects, later comes the ability to release them, using the whole hand, but by the end of the first year he is able to pick up small objects and pop them into his mouth, so he has to be watched since he is not overfussy about what he chews. It is part of his way of learning the nature of things, such as size, shape, hardness and texture.

As soon as an infant starts imitating words fairly easily, his mother generally believes he is talking, although true talking requires the use of words meaningfully, and he is not as yet really talking. However, it is a good thing that his mother thinks he is, for this gives her a great incentive in teaching him words. Long before the infant has any idea that he is naming mama, dada,

Come to Daddy

bunny, teddy, the average mother seizes on his babble sounds and invests them with meaning. By constantly naming herself "Mommy," and father "Daddy," she eventually teaches him to name things for himself. About the end of the first year, and with exceptionally advanced children at nine months, the baby may suddenly use his first word. This is probably a rather mutilated sound, to be true, rather remote from the adult version but nevertheless an articulate sound used with meaning. And this is a wonderful, great and momentous event in the development of your baby. He has begun to talk! And remember this achievement depends on you and goes back to the very first moment when you held him in your arms and spoke lovingly into his uncomprehending ears. Be proud of baby's achievement and be proud also of yours—it is an occasion for mutual congratulations!

I have spoken of the mother's investing her baby's babble syllables or vocables with meaning, of helping him to use the first words meaningfully by teaching him nursery words at first. It is fashionable nowadays among educated parents to reject with disgust the time-honored custom of using nursery words in this way to help an infant to talk. In a broadcast in which I advocated the use at a year old of this method of baby talk, or the child's "little language" as it has been called, I received a deluge of indignant letters from parents and schoolteachers who were genuinely shocked that a speech therapist of all people could recommend such harmful teaching methods. They obviously regarded the acceptance of nursery words as the primary cause of defective speech in children. These parents saw nothing inconsistent, incidentally, in allowing themselves to be called "Daddy" and "Mommy," or of referring to "baby," "teddy," or "golliwogg," which have no adult equivalent.

Of course to use baby talk when addressing a child, such as "Did Mommy's ikkle darling want an itsy-bitsy chockie before her din-din," is revolting at any time, and is a sentimental debasement of the human language. I certainly do not advocate this. However, the use of nursery words such as "choo-choo," "moo," "baa," derived from baby's own babbling, serves a good purpose at the right time. The most important thing at nine to twelve months is to encourage the small child to use articulate syllables with meaning, to communicate with words. It does not matter particularly what the sound is nearly so much as that the sound should be used consistently to refer to a toy, object or person. As soon as a child uses a syllable intelligently in this way, he is at one stroke lifted far above any other animal in creation. He thereby in fact qualifies as a human being, for only man can speak. Birds learn to imitate words and even nursery rhymes with extraordinary accuracy, but this is not speech because it has no meaning for the bird. The parakeet has no idea of the symbolism of any word or sentence he chirps forth.

Attempting to teach a one-year-old exact articulation is a waste of time. Try to teach him to say "dog," for instance, which necessitates the lifting of the tongue tip for "d" and a swift change to "o" and the lifting of the back of the tongue for "g." He cannot possibly manage this with his immature muscular co-ordination. Why not let him say "wow-wow," which he can manage with ease? The use of word pictures like "moo-cow," "baa-lamb," "choo-choo-train" and so forth is a great help in teaching the most important principle in learning to speak, which is that a vocal symbol stands for an object. He will soon discard the "moo," "baa" and "choo-choo" and use "cow," "lamb" and "train" when he is ready and especially if his parents discard the nursery props altogether by eighteen months. After all, you help baby with his first steps in walking, why not in talking?

It is extraordinary how hard it is to convince some parents that they may discourage their babies from trying to talk altogether by not using nursery words in this way at first. Going hand in hand with this intransigent attitude of course is a refusal to accept and understand baby's first crude attempts at naming things, so the poor mite may lose confidence in speaking and give up trying. The parents of one little girl declared that they would on no account allow Jane of nine months to say "bye-bye" but she must say "good-by," and not "Mommy and Daddy" but "Father and Mother." Since they endeavored to elicit these words from Jane and corrected all her spontaneous attempts at utterance and refused to understand her baby talk (the immature attempts at talking perfectly natural to every infant), this little mite grew so discouraged and frustrated she ceased to talk to her parents altogether. At two years she would only chatter freely to her grandmother, who was so old-fashioned that she had no notion of the new-fangled ideas concerning learning to talk. She understood baby talk and never drew attention to its deficiencies, and she also knew the arts of mothercraft and how to talk to little children—simply, sympatheti-

Naming Teddy

cally, matter-of-factly, using little words and sentences as she and Jane did odd jobs together round the house. Jane's parents realized the damage they were doing eventually, but Jane suffered a real setback and good, clear speech developed slowly as a result.

Rigid four-hourly feedings became the fashion this century and it was until recently considered a fearful breach of discipline to lift a wailing child up and pet him and give him a little snack between times. Now doctors and psychiatrists tell mothers to cuddle their babies when they need it and to feed them when they are hungry. This is no new idea but an incredibly old one. To my mind the idea that one should not use nursery words in teaching baby to talk is as unnatural as four-hourly feedings, and I look forward to the day when baby talk is once more discovered to be the right way of helping to get baby to talk.

II

From One to Two

Dawn's dew is on his tongue.
C. Day Lewis

It would be logical to assume that, once baby has started to talk, or at least to say a word or two, and grasped the idea of speech, he would now sail ahead and learn new words at a great pace and start stringing them together. But not a bit of it! In actual fact this is not the case and it is quite usual to find that the infant uses only a few more words in the half year from twelve to eighteen months. He may use three words at a year and only twenty or so at a year and a half. His understanding of speech certainly increases steadily, as witnessed by his ability in following more and more instructions. Obviously a lot more is going into the little head than is coming out of it.

The holdup in talking appears to be mainly due to his increased powers of locomotion, first by crawling or propelling himself along on his bottom and later by mastering the difficult skill of walking. This gets him places and is an exciting and absorbing occupation. Full of energy and with a pioneer zest for exploration he is into everything. It is much more practical and exciting to go and get what he wants rather than to ask for it. He feels no need for speaking and has little interest in learning words. He can imitate or echo words if asked but he does not use them himself. When he wants something out of reach of his prying fingers he will stretch out his hand and demand imperiously with some sort of vowel sound. He finds his own babble language quite satisfying and adequate; in fact, it takes him over what might be a frustrating time when he has something to talk about but no words with which to say it. Babbling reaches its height at eighteen months and is

Increased powers of locomotion

used as a sort of monologue when playing. This is the period of babble jargon or talking scribble, as it is sometimes called, because of its resemblance to a child's first pretense at writing. Some toddlers delight in jargon of this sort far more than others. In any case it should be encouraged for it prepares the way to fluent speech.

Listen to the youngster's anecdotes with sympathy and interest and suitable (though necessarily noncommittal) remarks—such as "Is that so?" and "Did it really?" and "Well, I never!" even though you may not have the remotest idea of what it is all about. For your child it is a lovely game of make-believe, this pretend talking, and it allows him to feel at one with you and to identify himself with the grown-ups, which, after all, is the stimulus in all children's make-believe. So loquacious are some infants at this stage, their jargon reflecting so realistically the melody and feelings portrayed in adult speech, that it is for all the world like a foreign language. A mother may feel baffled and helpless when unable to understand the stories, comments, jokes and complaints which

Doing a real job for Mummy

are so clearly distinguishable. She may feel happy and satisfied on the other hand, that her child is adapting well socially and will in time no doubt become an excellent raconteur.

Speech mimicry is only one facet of a small child's play between one and two. He loves to help mother about the house. Give him a duster or brush or a piece of dough, or allow him to help with the washing, and he will be blissfully happy, believing he is doing a real job and helping mommy. And remember, in these games it is important that you should go on talking to him, verbalizing the things you are doing together, translating activities into words, enlarging his experience with materials and language.

A toddler enjoys the sheer repetition of play at this age too. Everything is an exciting experiment into the nature of things. He will remain utterly absorbed for long spells, repeating the same game over and over again, such as putting bricks in a box and emptying them out again, or filling a pan with water and pouring it out. And of course dropping things out of the crib and carriage belongs to this phase too. Sometimes he appears to suffer from self-hypnosis and finds it difficult to cease when you want him to do something else. For instance, he may have to be lifted away bodily and carried off to a meal or a bath, most probably struggling and yelling. Here you can help him by giving him sufficient verbal warning of your intentions. Never bear down upon a child happily playing and whisk him away without any explanation, no matter how young he is. Help him to wind up his game by helping him to put away the toys, telling him as you do so of the next move, the next game in the bath. Let him help you turn on faucets, find the duck and fetch his pajamas. Give him something to visualize and hang on to. He lives in the immediate present and finds it hard to make transitions from one activity to another. Imagining the next move is not easy for him unless you can paint a word picture of it for him.

At twelve to fourteen months too, and most important, the toddler begins to enjoy the rhythms of nursery rhymes. He loves to be bounced on the knee to the accompaniment of a jingle, or swung astraddle father's foot to the chant of Ride a Cockhorse to Banbury Cross. Games of Ring Around the Rosy, Pat-a-cake, Pat-a-cake, This Little Pig Went to Market, Here We Go Round the Mulberry Bush and so forth, are immensely popular because they combine words, rhythm and movement. The youngster will go on demanding "More, more," long after you are exhausted. Such games are all useful language exercises since language is rhythmic and its rhythm has to be mastered before speech can be intelligible. We depend enormously upon stress and rhythm for our understanding of speech. If you change the stress of a polysyllabic word such as "phonograph" and stress perhaps the middle syllable it is less easy to recognize. Foreigners may master the vocabulary and syntax of English but remain virtually incomprehensible just because they retain the rhythm and melody of their native

So much to be learned about things!

language. As a weary delegate at an International Convention once remarked, "It is so much easier to understand French French and German German than French English and German English!"

Deaf children have to be given training in rhythm and movement, and tapping the stress of words and sentences helps them make their speech intelligible. It is a good plan, therefore, to start teaching nursery rhymes early. If you can sing to your baby this is fine and, if not, at least you can encourage your child to join in singing along with television programs, and to dance to music. Linking music and movement is a useful physical and intellectual exercise.

This is the time to introduce him to picture books with large clear pictures, and get him to point to the animals and toys and people as you name them. He will soon be joining in and naming them himself and chipping in with a word or two of the nursery rhymes. He is too young for stories as yet but you are paving the way for this and preparing him for the time when eventually he will be ready for formal education. Learning to know and love books cannot start too early, once he is able to recognize pictures.

At eighteen months our toddler is a dynamic youngster motivated by a superabundant and inexhaustible store of energy. He is a menace, in fact. He's never still and, because one doesn't know what he's going to do next, he's in need of constant supervision. His insatiable curiosity leads him to grab and handle things, investigate and explore, climb stairs and furniture. The contents of every drawer and cupboard are his prey, and boxes, cans and bottles must be opened, emptied, tasted and scattered. This is not naughtiness. Naughtiness is only an adult's interpretation of behavior which is inconvenient and troublesome to himself. I am no believer in the existence of original sin, though perhaps some infants have more devil in them than others. Your child behaves this way because he has to. This is the only way to learn all about things—all those things that as adults we now take for granted.

We forget that as children we had to learn in the same way as our own child. There is so much to be learned about the things a toddler handles: the shape, size, weight, and the difference between hard and soft, fluid and solid, color and smell and taste. By scrambling onto chairs and tables and falling off them, he learns to measure height and distance as well as how to climb and the hard facts about the force of gravity. It is learning the hard way for a mother and she may well sigh for those blissful days when her treasure lay angelic and helpless in his carriage all day. The only solution to those trials and tribulations is to provide him with plenty of occupation and suitable play material. Give him a sand tray and if he spills some it is easy enough to sweep up. Don't fuss too much about a mess. He will be happy for hours pouring sand into different-sized containers and pouring it out again. Or give

Take the stroller along

him water and pots and pans in the sink; or soap and water and his socks and let him get on with it. Take him on walks too and let him walk off some of his rambunctious animal energy that way. But take his stroller along. He often becomes tired all of a sudden, really tired and needing to rest weary legs, and his whining to be carried is no whim. His legs won't carry him further.

After eighteen months the child begins to talk a bit more. He no longer shakes his head but can say "No," though not "Yes," which he indicates with a nod for some months to come. He no longer just names objects but takes an important step forward when he uses them as one-word sentences, the inflections of the voice supplying the missing words and expressing interrogation, statement and command. He begins to run two words together and uses them as little clichés in the right context: for example, "tidow" for "sit down"; "doorsut" for "shut the door"; "orgone" for "all gone." There is no appreciation of the exact definition of words nor of the use of names according to set rules of classification, such as the genus and species as in the case of chair and armchair. Any man is called "Daddy," to the embarrassment of mother, and there is no realization at first that "Daddy" refers to a particular man, the father. The same does not hold true for the baby's use of "Mommy," since there can only be one mother for him. This link is so strong that he makes no mistakes about identity in her case.

The child has his own system of classification, however, though not the conventional one. It is fascinating to work out what the common characteristic is that he selects when giving the same name to totally dissimilar articles. For instance, one child had a special word for everything with handles. "Birdie" may apply to everything that flies—an airplane, a butterfly or a leaf blown by the wind. "Moon" may be anything round—a penny, a biscuit, a plate or a saucer. Until he has sorted the problem out and discovered that everything has its own name he naturally remains very much restricted in vocabulary. The realization dawns slowly in most cases but we have on record the famous case of Helen Keller, who was stricken with total deafness and blindness at nineteen months. Her governess, who came to teach her at the age of six, began to teach her the manual alphabet, "talking into her hand as we talk into a baby's ear." In this way the small Helen learned a number of words, but she confused words such as mug, milk, water. At last Miss Sullivan took her with her mug to a pump down the garden. She let cold water pour over one hand while spelling water in her other hand. Helen dropped the mug and stood transfixed. A new light came into her face. She spelled water several times. Then she dropped on the ground and asked for its name, touched the pump and the trellis, and suddenly turned and asked Miss Sullivan her name. All the way back to the house the child was highly excited, learning the names of all the objects she touched so that in a few hours she had added thirty words to her vocabulary.

We do not notice this all-important step in learning to talk happening so dramatically in normal children, but one day toward the end of the second year parents realize that their youngster is suddenly smitten with an insatiable desire for learning what things are. He starts demanding, "What's that?" perpetually. Quite suddenly the toddler has developed an absolute craze for collecting names. It can be trying for mother and father at times and often he seems to be asking, "What's that?" just to attract attention, and forgets the names as soon as he has learned and repeated them. But actually he has a keen delight in learning new words and, though he may forget some of them, the majority stick. Proof of this fact is that by the age of two he is probably using two hundred or more words.

His vocabulary now increases at an astonishing rate and so does his chattering. He has arrived at last at the vital stage of "speech readiness," the time when the small child learns his mother tongue most readily and easily. And of course it is necessary to pour speech into his ears and give him the opportunity to imitate and learn. Now he begins to forsake his babble jargon, and as he plays around the house, trailing mother, he begins to verbalize what he is doing, and the many months of listening to mother begin to produce results. The new words he learns begin to fall into patterns and to form sentences. Speech is far from perfect, grammatical constructions are weird to say the least, and words are mutilated and often difficult to recognize—so much so that his mother is often the only one who can understand him. But thank goodness she does, and he is spared the frustration of not being understood. He is totally unaware that he is not speaking clearly and thinks his speech is fine, and no doubt he is very proud of his new accomplishment. Never let him lose his confidence, therefore, in this marvelous new skill. It is far more satisfying to him and important to his development than any of the other great feats at this age, such as managing to run or to climb up and down stairs unaided.

This reminds me of Michael, who was brought to me at the age of four by his anxious mother because he was not yet talking. Michael's mother was really devoted to him and had never left him or gone out to work leaving him with neighbors or in a day nursery. He was a good, obedient little boy, very shy but never any trouble, and excellent at amusing himself. He understood everything said to him, and in every way, as far as I could see, was a perfectly normal child—except that perhaps he seemed a little too good, and of course he wasn't talking. At first, I could not imagine what had gone amiss with his speech development. Then one day after I had been playing with him I gave him a toy to take home and he ran out to show his mother, his little face radiant with delight and eagerness to share his joy with her. But she just glanced at him and then turned to me, asking, "Is he ready to go now?" I saw the light fade from the little fellow's face and the disappointment.

This small incident gave me a valuable clue. Tactful questioning following this lead gave me a quite different and unexpected picture of life at home. His mother told me she was very reserved and kept herself apart from the neighbors. She was obviously too inhibited to talk freely even to her little boy. She confessed she thought it was silly to talk to a baby who couldn't understand, and so she had never done so. She was, in fact, far too self-conscious to talk to Michael. I had to explain that no child would talk without his mother talking to him continuously, for this is just how a child imitates and learns words. After this she used to come into my clinic and watch us play together on the floor: the toys planned all sorts of mischief, and were caught, scolded and punished. Michael became very aggressive in his play, showing that he had been far too repressed. He also lost his shyness with me and other strangers.

Michael's mother announced after her first session of play therapy that she now saw exactly where she had been wrong, and she confessed she had never played like this with him. Either she had been busy about the house or she sat knitting and sewing while Michael played nearby—on his own. She now began to talk to him and to play with him, and quite a change came over her as well as over Michael, who suddenly began to chatter. Another thing I discovered was that Michael was not "without a single word" when he first came to see me, but that he had a number of poorly articulated names for things, and his mother had never recognized these as speech. So she had never encouraged him in his shy attempts at utterance. When at last she did, he soon became a voluble youngster, but like the little Jane I mentioned earlier, he did not speak well until about six years old. We never corrected his speech, though; we were too happy just to release the speech that had been dammed up for so long and we knew that school at five would do the rest.

There was no real language difficulty with this little boy, just a lack of stimulation through the vital listening period. You may ask what part his father played in this child's life, and couldn't he have helped? Apart from the fact that he too was a silent man, our social system is such that a father sees very little of his baby at first—he rushes off to work early in the morning and generally returns after the baby is tucked in bed at night. It is upon mother that the full responsibility of teaching baby to talk falls. Father's contribution is added later on.

I have mentioned the toddler's poor pronunciation, but of what does this really consist? Chiefly the substitution of one consonant for another—examples would be: "tat" for "cat"; "jeg" for "leg"; "fee" for "three"; "tee" for "see." Though some proud mothers swear their children spoke from the very first with perfect clarity and never talked "baby talk," I do not really believe them. I attribute it to understandable maternal pride and an untrained ear. I have myself never heard a two-year-old with perfect pronunciation. It is normal for a small child to make these mistakes, and it is quite wrong, in my opinion, for parents to try to correct them. I examined the two-year-old daughter of a doctor the other day. Mary's father was concerned that the child could not say "cat" but said "tat," and persisted in saying "dod" for "dog," however much he corrected her. Yet he wanted me to give her speech therapy! He had taught her to imitate "fish" correctly after correcting her "sis" a hundred times but she continued to say "sis" whenever she referred to fish spontaneously. The mother herself was not worried, but since father was a doctor, she thought he must know all about these things. Fortunately I was able to reassure Mary's parents in time, before any damage was done. I stressed the fact that there was no need for correction and the child would imitate speech correctly when she was ready to do so.

Another characteristic of this baby speech or "lalling" is that two consonants together are also a difficulty and at first only one of a pair is pronounced. For a long time the toddler says "poon" instead of "spoon," "carf" instead of "scarf," or "cool" for "school." Also compound words, not surprisingly, get a bit mixed up and syllables may be reversed, consonants rearranged or omitted. "Bikist" for biscuit is a common example; also "bakif" for "basket" and "efelant" for "elephant," and I have even heard "runny babbit." Every child produces his own delightful versions. Heather, aged two, said "hockle-bockle" meaning "hot-water bottle," "mardapane" for "marmalade" and "hop-grasser" for "grasshopper." I asked her once to say "mosquito, rhinoceros, gentleman, and hippopotamus" just as an experiment, and the nearest she could get was "mosspeeto, rhinosteros, genkum, and hippotomusk!"

The youngster does not know that he is not imitating correctly what he hears and it is most unkind and tactless to laugh at him. You yourself would resent having your oddities of speech pointed out to you, and don't believe you haven't any—we all have! You should enjoy these amusing variants of adult speech and you will do so when you realize how difficult pronunciation is for the little child, and how marvelously well he gets his little tongue round real tongue twisters, and makes the good job of it that he does, all things being considered.

I kept a record of my daughters' queer pronunciations, their delightful anecdotes and amusing remarks. I only wish I had noted down many more than I did. One forgets so soon, and they grew up so fast. However, in reading these old records I can capture a little of those magic years which fly past far too quickly. Reading, for example, "my jegs lake," how vividly I recall Heather, with scarlet cheeks and black hair flying, clinging to my hand, and charging the "ups and downs," as the old Roman mounds on our common are called—beyond the "Baa-lamb" trees and the pond, the "Silver Cup." These are the names known to everyone for the places where the children from our village play.

So enjoy your child's talking to the full. It is enough to talk to him clearly and slowly for him to copy you when he is mature enough to do so. There is never any need to inflict upon him the misery of tackling a thing too soon and before he is old enough to learn to do what you want.

III
From Two to Three

The artless prattle of a child
Drives nearly everybody wild;
And who that for an hour beguiled
   A babe however clever
For all the riches of the rich
Would undertake a life in which
They lived at that exacting pitch
   Ten hours a day for ever?

A. P. Herbert

It can be said that the child embarks upon his third year equipped
with the full *readiness* to learn to talk. This enables him, during
this year, to obtain a marvelous proficiency and fluency in speech.
Studies of the growth of vocabulary during the third year show
that at the age of two and a half most children have doubled the
number of words they used at two. At three they have doubled the
number of words they had at two and a half. At two years a
forward child may use a hundred words, at two and a half four
hundred words and at three years eight hundred words. As the
child grows older he does not learn at quite this astonishing speed.
But between two and a half and four and a half it is said that he
learns about fifty new words a month. The ability to learn and use
words is extraordinary in the preschool years, to say the least. But,

if by some misfortune a child misses his chance of learning speech at this time, either from lack of stimulation or perhaps undiscovered deafness, it is much more difficult to make up later for his bad start. It is not quite so easy after four to learn language.

For example a little boy whose parents were deaf and dumb and communicated by signs himself "talked" with signs but failed to learn to speak through sheer deprivation of the opportunity to listen to speech in a wordless home. His mother and father kept very much to themselves and had little contact with neighbors and the child was not sent to nursery school until four years old. When he came to the speech clinic at five years his use and comprehension of speech were so limited we thought at first he too must be deaf. But this was not so; it was just that he had not learned to *listen* in early childhood nor to link words and meanings. His speech, even with special training, developed far more slowly than that of the toddler and was not normal until after the age of seven.

After two the child is less restless and better able to amuse himself. He talks a great deal to himself as he plays. Much of it is not very sensible but such egocentric monologues are nevertheless excellent practice in speaking. He may chant his own sort of Volga boat song to aid him in his work, such as "John bang, Daddy bang, brick bang, teddy bang." Heather had a religious phase after eavesdropping upon the devotions of a clergyman who stayed with us. "God bless teddy, God bless dolly, God bless me, God bless birdie, God bless horsie," not to mention "Bless my soul, where's my ball; bless my soul, where's my coat; bless my soul, where's my shoe?" As this phase descended on her before the departure of our visitor it caused the poor man some embarrassment.

Another interesting feature is that the small child is often heard whispering to himself as if savoring the feel of the sounds on his tongue. He loves rhythmic movements and these often accompany his play, banging, bouncing, rocking and swinging his legs, and of course, he can now probably recite nursery rhymes with a little prompting.

Make-believe games develop greatly during this third year as the child's imagination increases and is not tied so firmly—as it was earlier—to things he could see and handle at the moment. Games can be played without any props. It is not necessary to have a doll's tea set for tea. Bricks or stones or even empty gestures will do. The shopping game is very popular, the child going off to buy mother a dozen eggs, a pound of sugar, a package of cookies, trotting to and fro with his imaginary purchases, and learning words all the time. Too many toys, in fact, stifle a child's imagination and do not make him really happy. He needs help from his parents at first, however, to develop his powers of imagination in play. The toddler does not invent the shopping game, for example; his mother suggests it to him.

Heather, whose birthday falls soon after Christmas, enjoyed her Christmas presents but was overcome by another twenty presents on her birthday. She solved the problem in her own way. She lined up all her birthday presents in their wrappings down one side of the bedroom and refused to look at them again for several weeks. She had learned to amuse herself with bricks, stroller, teddy, sandbox and "housework" and new toys bored her.

Between two and two and a half the toddler makes great advances in motor development which have their influence on speech and social adaptation. Much better hand, eye and finger co-ordination develops. If you ask the two-year-old to imitate waggling the thumb with fist clenched, he responds by opening and shutting his whole fist. At two and a half he can manage this difficult feat of isolating the movement of the thumb from the whole hand. With this progress he can now handle objects with greater skill and build a tower of bricks because he is able to aim accurately and manage the release of each brick without upsetting the whole edifice. He also learns to scribble with a pencil, to string large wooden beads and to unwrap a piece of candy. He eats less messily too, and gets the spoon in and out of his mouth without twisting it and spilling the contents. He can now undo buttons with precise fingers, though as yet not manage to do them up. As Sally said when asked by a visitor whether she could do up the buttons of her coat, "No, but I can do them undone."

With the great improvement in motor skill, mother should cash in on a program of "do it yourself." Encourage your child to brush his teeth, wash his hands and face, and undress and so on. He loves doing things for himself if given a chance, and, though he may not do them very well and leave the finishing touches to you, it is vitally important that he should be allowed to assert his independence in this way.

This is the time to loosen the apron strings. The utter physical dependence of a child upon his mother must be severed and this is the age at which to achieve this objective painlessly. It is a necessary step in the child's growing up, and you must help him make it or there will be a great deal of trouble later on when he has to leave you to go to school—and, indeed, throughout his whole life. The mother who waits on her child hand and foot because she wants to keep him a baby a little longer does her child a great hurt and no kindness. Devotion which stifles the growth of individuality and independent personality is no devotion in reality, no evidence of selflessness but selfishness. Try not to overprotect your child therefore. Teach him to look after himself and bring him up to be self-sufficient and independent. He will love you no less for this, but rather more.

Emancipation from the mother and the gain in emotional maturity is reflected in the gain in speech maturity, and lalling or baby talk is gradually left behind. When a child persists in using babyish speech, the reason usually is that he has not managed to break from his babyish dependence upon his mother. This can scarcely be due to his failure to grow up but hers in failing to let him.

The advances in motor dexterity and emotional maturity are

reflected in the child's speech, which grows progressively clearer during the second year. Pronunciation improves enormously and most consonants are mastered; and the substitutions which were characteristic formerly are now a thing of the past. Many children, however, still lisp, substituting a "th" sound for "s," and this is so common at five or even six that it is nothing to worry about. If it persists beyond this age it can be an indication of emotional immaturity.

Two consonants together now begin to make their appearance, once all the consonants are mastered. Often by the age of three the youngster has ceased to say "pum" for "plum," "pay" for "play" or "back" for "black," though "s" plus a consonant may still cause difficulty as when a child says "poon" for spoon," etc.

The toddler is still pretty deficient in language but begins to use more parts of speech—prepositions for example. "In" and "on" are used correctly at two years and are a good gauge of language development. "Under" and "behind" are more difficult and are not used until three or later. Pronouns are also coming along. The first are "me" or "you," which are distinguished at two years when the child stops referring to himself by his name. The difference between "I" and "me" is quite difficult to grasp, however, and these pronouns may not be used correctly till three or three and a half, and only when the child really recognizes himself as an independent individual. Plurals appear early but all follow the general rule of adding "s" and irregular plurals result, such as— "sheeps," "mouses," and "mans." Past tenses are conjugated again according to the general rule of adding "ed," the child saying "me runned," "he eated," and "me seed."

One of the most delightful and entertaining characteristics of the speech of the child who is almost three is the ability to invent names for objects whose true names are not known. A bright child shows extraordinary ingenuity in inventing analogies drawn from his existing vocabulary. Classic examples are "hair-flames" for curls, "mouth-brush" for mustache, "tinkle chest of drawers" for piano, all recorded by Stern. I have noted "stick-ears" for horns, and "grass-scissors" for shears. Of course adult language is full of such analogies—pigtails, looking glass, screwdriver—and one wonders whether children were not responsible for these contributions to the language originally. At least these inventions show the marvelous logic with which the child's mind works.

At two and a half or thereabouts a child stops nodding his head and starts saying "yes." I regret to say, however, that "no" is still heard more frequently! Toward the end of the third year the child enters a "difficult" stage and behavior problems begin to rear their ugly heads for the first time. The fact that the boy refers to himself no longer as "John" but "me" is significant and indicates an increasing awareness of himself as an important person with a will of his own, and the possibilities of exerting it. No longer is your small son or daughter docile and obedient. Not only "no" but "won't" is commonly heard, and moreover asserted and maintained. This is not altogether sheer willfulness but often timidity. The child is increasingly aware of himself and his own smallness and inadequacy in relation to the big and often alarming outside world. He is not very sure of himself these days, in fact, and his behavior shows strange and unaccountable swings between dependence and independence. He may suddenly become very shy with strangers and create a scene when mother wants to leave him with father or a relative for a few hours. On the other hand he may set out alone on a voyage of discovery down the street and get lost. He wants to be caressed and cuddled one moment and rejects holding your hand to cross the street at another.

Mother at this time may be disconcerted by her child's sudden passionate preference for father, but may utilize this development and allow him to handle difficulties which arise, and not allow herself to be piqued by father's just assertion that he finds young John "no trouble at all." The devotion a youngster feels for father is true hero worship for a marvelous being who knows everything and can do anything. Motherlike, I did not realize how deep

Heather's love and dependence upon her father were until after one of his frequent departures abroad I found her sobbing over an album of holiday photographs. "What is the matter?" I asked her. "I'm tired of only you, I want my Daddy," she replied.

Difficulty over meals often crops up. The child suddenly discovers that not only are mushes of spinach and rice pudding revolting but that he need not eat them. He refuses his hitherto favorite foods, but with fanatical conservatism he also refuses to taste any other delicacies with which you try to tempt him. The old nursery game, "A little one for teddy, and a big one for Daddy," may help, or a story manufactured for the occasion. One thing is fatal and that is to force him to eat if he cannot be reasoned with, because complete unreasonableness is uppermost in these crises. It is far better to let him be and allow him to leave his dinner if he wants to. He will probably make up for it at the next meal when he is hungry. But make sure you don't spoil his appetite with cookies and ice cream.

The best plan is to treat him like a sensible human being. Consult him over the luncheon menu before hand and let him help to prepare it, and to set the table. Allow him to eat with the family and give him a small helping and let him ask for more if he wants it. I can remember the anxiety to this day of having lunch with my grandmother on Sundays and knowing I could not eat the heaped plate of food set in front of me. I am sure I could not have been more than three at that time.

It is important not to turn meals into a battleground from which mother has to retreat defeated. If John simply won't eat, let him not eat. It is disastrous to let him know that his refusal of food upsets you. Far from feeling concerned the little tyrant will revel in using his power as a weapon. He will remember one victory and work up to another at the next meal.

It is extraordinary to what lengths child and mother will go. A child was admitted to our hospital recently because she had refused to eat altogether and her mother was on the verge of a nervous breakdown. Sarah was not even asked to eat anything in the children's ward and no pressure whatever was put on her. At first she scowled from her bed at mealtimes for a couple of days. Then, of her own free will, she joined the other children at the table and began to eat voraciously anything and everything put before her.

A little one for Teddy

A friend of mine, a schoolteacher, had very strict views on child training and produced a model daughter who was toilet trained night and day by eighteen months, could speak beautifully at two, and whose manners were impeccable. Then suddenly at two and a half, without any warning, the revolt set in. Mary began wetting herself every half hour and she refused her food. She was made to sit at a table one whole afternoon and eat her rice pudding grain by grain. "I would not let her defy me," said Mary's mother. "She ate every scrap in the end." "And what happened at supper-time?" I asked with great interest. "She was sick," replied Mary's mother. "Perhaps I shouldn't have been so strict. She may not have been feeling well all the time." I thought I detected a sign of weakening. When I met her a few weeks later I inquired tact-fully how Mary's appetite now was. Mary had emerged triumphant it seemed. She was living on ambrosia—chocolate, ice cream, bread and cheese, apples and plenty of milk. "A perfectly ade-quate diet, the doctor says," announced her mother defensively. And Mary had apparently stopped wetting herself.

Toilet training may also become a problem in the daytime. Whereas it did not matter earlier, mother may become anxious about accidents after two years, expecting higher standards from the youngster. Very early toilet training is seldom successful. A child may be trained at four months to eliminate after meals and to be clean at nine months, but this early training invariably breaks down later. The feeling of guilt and anxiety which the child may then experience, as a result of his mother's disappointment and an-noyance, can become really harmful. In training your little child it is helpful to understand this, and also that in development of the control of the anal muscle, contraction develops before re-laxation. The same sequence is evident in the baby's ability to grasp with the hand before he learns how to release. The toddler may therefore actually go through a phase of withholding a motion when placed on the toilet and then earn a scolding for soiling himself when released. If you understand the actual difficulty, which your child certainly does not, only being aware of the frustration and disgrace, then you can handle the situation sym-pathetically. What has toilet training to do with speech develop-ment you may ask, and have we not strayed rather far from the purpose of this book? Not at all. Toilet training is not achieved generally until the youngster can tell you he wants to go to the toilet. Therefore, he should be taught and allowed to use some simple nursery terms so that he can anticipate and give warning of his needs.

All aspects of development in these early years are tied up with motor development and speech. This is very obvious in play with other children. During the second half of the third year, that is between two and a half and three, interest in other children

Submissive with older children

grows but the toddler has no idea of co-operative play. Though generally full of admiration for older children and behaving with amusing submissiveness toward them, toddlers react to each other quite differently. They may eye each other nervously while clinging to their mothers or take their toys to different parts of the room and play alone. If expected to share toys they refuse and grab and push. In fact, their only idea of contact is a physical one, often hugging or pushing each other around until separated.

Two toddlers confronted by each other seem to react according to the mood of the moment. Heather was taken out to tea with Judy and her little six-month-old brother. Heather took along a favorite book which she refused to let Judy touch, so Judy would not let her play with her toys, but Heather did not mind this, being fascinated by the baby. Eventually Judy, tired of playing by herself and the lack of attention, picked up a building brick and proceeded to rub it all over Heather, saying, "I'm busy— I'm ironing."

Heather thought this funny and laughed, but when Judy began to iron out her face, Judy's mother intervened, saying, "You're hurting Heather, stop it. That's enough, Judy."

Thereupon Judy threw her arms round Heather and kissed her. Heather promptly pushed her off and kicked her.

"Why did you do that?" I asked horrified.

"Judy *bited* me," said Heather in tones of righteous indignation.

Soon after this episode Heather demanded loudly and insistently to be taken home. When we took our leave as gracefully as I could manage in the circumstances, Judy's mother said to Heather unwisely, "You'll come and see us again soon, won't you, dear?"

"No, I won't," retorted Heather.

On the way home I told Heather I did not think she had been very polite and ended with the pious hope that when Judy came to tea with us Heather would let her play with the beautiful doll's house Daddy had made her before going away.

"I won't."

"Well, then you will have to play in your bedroom."

"Yes, I take my dolly's house with me and I lock the door."

Children cannot play with each other until language has developed sufficiently for an interchange of remarks or for one child, at least, to indicate to his playmate what he is playing at, and so direct operations. Communication is, in fact, essential for co-operative play, but is also dependent upon the ability to play constructively and realistically. At two the small child is satisfied with heaping bricks together and scattering them, filling cans with sand and spilling the contents. By three he is beginning to build towers with bricks and will tell you afterward he has made a house or garage, though it may have little resemblance to anything. Now, a brick will no longer make do for an airplane or truck and the child likes to have a real toy to push about. He really appreciates his toys and gets a lot of fun out of them. It is not until over three years that he can visualize a real play program and join in with another child. Even so, games at this time may be for the most part active. Little boys especially are likely to charge around chasing each other, working up to a frenzy of excitement, playing trains or cowboys and Indians. They are capable of sensible games with trains, building bricks, toy soldiers or farm animals, however, and should be encouraged to follow these pursuits indoors for the sake of peace. Little girls generally show the imprint of their femininity in their play, and are less wild than boys. They enjoy domestic games such as tea parties with dolls and playing families, feeding, bathing and dressing, and putting their babies to bed.

IV

Three to Four

I know a person small—
She keeps ten million serving-men
Who get no rest at all!
She sends 'em abroad on her own affairs
From the second she opens her eyes—
One million Hows, two million Wheres
And seven million Whys!

Rudyard Kipling

Three years old is perhaps the most charming age the small child can be. The crises and scenes that blew up so unexpectedly a few months back and nearly drove you to distraction are, as a result of wise management, a thing of the past. The youngster is now a more stable and reasonable little being. The next nine months are a period of consolidation in which the crude skills he acquired one after the other at breakneck speed are more or less perfected. The child is now a co-operative little person, much more obedient and even anxious to please, and a real companion —one you can talk to and who talks back. At first he had difficulty in establishing his independence and breaking the physical dependence on his mother. This brought on the battles with authority. Now he can look after himself quite a bit and can let his mother leave him, secure in the knowledge that it is not for long and she will be back soon. The safety and stability of his home, the love of his parents to cloak him are just as necessary as ever, but the real difference lies in the fact of his not needing so much physical attention and protection.

Gesell has said that "two acquires words and three uses them," describing very neatly the change that takes place in speaking round about three years old. Just as there was at two years old, there is a sudden mania again for information and a veritable plague of questions. But at three it is a very different kind of inquisition to which the youngster submits one. It is no longer a hunger for names that keeps his tongue wagging, but a burning zeal for explanations. Like the Elephant's Child, he is full of "satiable curtiosity" and that means he asks ever so many questions. Why, what, when, where, how, who and again why? The child is no longer content with just observing the world about him. He no longer accepts anything at its face value. He wants to know about things: where they come from, who made them, how they work and why, why, why, all the day. He cannot understand and obtain insight into how things work without the language to do so. He needs you to give him explanations so that he can understand, so that he can put two and two together and arrive at an answer. This is the dawn of reasoning, which is almost entirely dependent on language. This stage is immensely important in your child's mental development and, as always, he is dependent upon your teaching and the simple language in which you teach him.

Sometimes it is hard to be patient when the little inquisitor pesters you so, like some mechanical robot demanding "Why?" every time you pause for breath. But never scold him or tell him to stop or be quiet. Let him poke his nose into everything! Remember what happened to the Elephant's Child when they spanked him and refused to answer his questions. When you are beside yourself with exasperation you can always turn the tables on him and ask him questions. Ask him, "What do you think?

You tell me." He often gives surprisingly sensible answers or may surprise you with the utter naïveté of his explanation. The following is an example of the kind of conversation one gets involved in. Heather always woke up early and scrambled into my bed long before breakfast and before I was ready to wake up. Imagine coping with this at six in the morning:

"Who made the Sudan?"

"I don't know."

"Why?"

"Why, what?"

"Why don't you know?"

"Because it was there before men came."

"Who made it?"

"God did."

"Why?"

"Because He wanted it there."

"Why?"

"Because He thought it was a good idea."

"Why?"

"Because He wanted a hot, sunny place to go to when He was fed up with rain and fog."

"Why?"

"Well, don't you like the sun better than rain?"

"Yes"—pause for thought—"Who made God?"

"He made Himself."

"Why?"

"You must ask Him yourself."

"I don't know Him."

"Yes, you do. He's the Person you say your prayers to." Then taking the offensive I asked, "What do you think He looks like?"

Long pause for thought. At last, "God knows."

There is no need to go into scientific dissertations when answering a small child's questions. In fact the simpler your answers the better and they need not be any the less straightforward for their simplicity. The questions about everything on earth, sacrosanct and outrageous, about birth, God, elimination, the difference between boys and girls, all are prompted by pure curiosity and an entirely innocent desire to know, just as innocent as his questions about "many things: of shoes—and ships—and sealing-wax—of cabbages—and kings." Always answer his questions as directly and honestly as possible. He is quick to detect embarrassment or evasion in your replies and he should never be allowed to get the idea that certain topics are naughty and forbidden. This may create an unhealthy preoccupation with them. If your child wants to know how babies are made and how he was made, tell him "in Mommy's tummy," and not "found under a gooseberry bush." He accepts such an explanation matter-of-factly. It is not the incredible miracle that it is for you. Everything, to him, is credible and he thinks nothing more of such information than, for instance, of being told that a chick comes out of an egg. And you should be able to talk as dispassionately about babies as you can about chicks. Besides, if you hedge or talk about gooseberry bushes, he will find you out in the end and mark it up against you. Let him have the facts straight from the start. It is the only way and the right way.

I remember being told by the housemaid that my baby sister was found under a gooseberry bush in the garden. Even at three and a quarter this struck me as very odd indeed. So I asked my aunt. "Dear little Helen," said she, "was brought by the doctor last night in his black bag." I then went and asked my mother. "Helen came out of my tummy," she said. *Et tu, Brute!* This was the end! The worst nonsense of all! I knew now that they were all concealing something from me. What and why?

When he is not asking questions the three- or four-year-old is a garrulous little creature full of gossip. He endeavors to explain things for himself and his observations and conclusions are so wide of the mark one realizes how little insight he actually has. His reasoning at this age is limited really to nothing more than the glimmering of an awareness that things bear some relation to one another. Eva Stern of three and a half kissed a chair and her father remarked, "The chair will laugh now."

"It can't laugh," said Eva.

"Why not?"

"It hasn't any teeth."

John, startled by the cat which jumped from a window sill behind him, started belaboring the poor animal.

"Why are you hitting the cat?"

"He's a bad cat."

"Why? He didn't touch you."

"He didn't tell me him coming."

Heather announced one day with satisfaction, "I know what a joke is."

"What is it then?"

"A joke's a laugh."

Small children, of course, do not realize that inanimate objects, animals, birds and toys do not behave like human beings. This accounts for Eva's odd remark above and also John's. Heather, when three, enjoyed building a snowman and when he was complete, resplendent with cabbage leaf hat, Daddy's pipe and stone buttons down his manly front, Heather begged him to talk to her.

"Talk to me, 'nowman, *please* talk to me," she pleaded. But he didn't and her eyes filled with tears of disappointment. Quickly I made some kind of remark in a gruff snowman sort of voice. Immediately she laughed and in a moment was impersonating him herself. And how much more fun we both had that morning in the snow and sun as a result of my playing make-believe, than if I had said, "Don't be silly, he's only snow. He can't talk!"

Certainly to play with small children and enter their world of mixed fantasy and fact, to know when they need facts and when fiction, requires a sensitive intuition and a quick imagination. It is a great art in which we all fail at times, since as we grow up most of us lose touch with the magic world of childhood.

Children see no inconsistency therefore in tales in which engines, teddy bears, golliwoggs, horses, cats, mice and birds speak, think and behave like real children. Stories are immensely popular when they concern little incidents which a child can

Talk to me, 'nowman

relate to his own experience. Well-illustrated storybooks with simple language can now be read to him right through. He no longer grows restless and wants to see the next page before you have started the first. Teach your child to love books from the start and to treat them well, to be loved for the treasures they contain. The simplest story, besides, teaches a child new words, constructions and ideas. Because the written and formalized account read from a storybook by mother is really so different from the fluid loose language of conversation, it is undoubtedly an aid in teaching language. A child who has been read to, as well as talked to, will find learning to read much easier than the child who has not, and does not know what to expect from books or his first reader. With the retentive memory which the youngster of three or four possesses, he soon knows whole books by heart and will complete sentences for you and quickly detect any attempt to cut and shorten the story. He loves the same story over and over again, and, best of all, he loves stories which contain a great deal of repetition. A child can listen to a story like that of "Little Black Sambo" hundreds and hundreds of times without ever growing tired of it. This explains the popularity, the *raison d'être* in fact, of the age-old narrative rhymes like "This Is the House That Jack Built," "Old Mother Hubbard," and the stories of "Henny, Penny," "Billy Goat Gruff" and "The Three Little Pigs." Such ageless classics, I veritably believe, were invented long ago by grannies sitting by the fire in their rocking chairs and catering exactly to the needs of small grandsons and granddaughters!

These ancient rhymes and tales are considered old-fashioned by many parents I know. Modern children's tales reflect the adult restlessness and desire for constant change and variety, chasing their tails in an effort to escape boredom. But this isn't what children like most, although if you give them nothing else they won't know any better. I especially deplore the picture books which display nine or a dozen small, overcrowded pictures on one page with badly worded captions beneath, describing one fantastic event after another. Such narratives give the child no time to assimilate, filling his head with a jumbled confusion of sights and sounds. This does not mean I disapprove of comics. I cannot bear them myself but children love the pictures and following a tale pictorially without words. This is another thing altogether and I am no spoilsport after all. But we are discussing the best way to teach children language, and reading literature to your child—not trash but well-written stories—and reading them over and over again, is a marvelous way of obtaining results. Compare the Beatrix Potter classics for their charm and beauty, poetry and interest, humanity and humor, to many of the books which flood the market nowadays and you will get my meaning, I think. And while I am on the subject of entertainment for your child, let me stress here and now that however good television programs for children may be, they can never replace the teaching a child needs directly from his parents: the need to listen and to be listened to in these early years.

The small child's first introduction to books of course should be to picture books—picture books of animals and alphabet picture books. He does not need a story at eighteen months, but at two years he is ready to listen longer to what you read and this leads on to the storybooks we have been discussing.

It is interesting to know a little about how the toddler recognizes pictures at first. You must realize that he needs training in looking and in listening. I remember being amazed that the six-year-old son of my Sudanese cook literally could not make head or tail of a comic my five-year-old daughter showed him. He held the page upside down, then sideways, and was even more puzzled when I righted it for him, naming the pictures in Arabic. He had never seen a picture book before and the strange shapes and colors on the paper meant nothing to him at all.

The tiny child of eighteen months to two years learns to recognize only outlines at first—and will learn to name some animals correctly, though he will confuse a goat and a cow and a horse even at three years. He identifies shapes by some particular feature which strikes him forcibly and helps his classification in exactly the same way as with actual objects. You remember I said any man may be "Daddy" and anything round "moon." Thus any picture of an animal with four legs may be a horse, because it is the legs which are significant, not the hump or neck of a camel, the beard of a goat or the horns of a cow, which are the points of significance for us.

I have an alphabet picture book with which I test these three-year-olds. Mothers of children with rather poor speech often tell me their children do not recognize pictures because of the mistakes they make. But they are recognizing outlines and shapes in their own way. In this book there is a picture of a hat which most children call a cake and some a tortoise. The duck, chicken and blackbird are all "birdie" by reason of their having two legs. There is a picture of a knife which is sometimes called a dagger, or a boat or even a scrubbing brush! On one page there is a picture of a dragonfly, an earwig, a ballet dancer and an easel— all have a lot of projections and one enterprising small boy called them all "pider" (spider). A mother who does not realize why the child is making these extraordinary mistakes may be really worried as to the extent of his intelligence. And if she does not understand his efforts at pronunciation, which may consist only of vowels, all consonants being omitted, she may be really convinced that her child isn't talking at all. This is often why she has brought him to see me, of course. Naming pictures correctly will gradually teach a child to notice differences and details. This is important because it lays the foundation for word recognition and recognition of the differences in the shapes of letters, though perhaps the average child is not capable of this until he is five or so.

Besides enjoying listening to stories, the three-year-old's imagination is so vivid and lively that he is able to invent quite good stories of his own. Many of these may start off realistically enough with an account of an actual event and end up fantastically with no relation to truth at all. Be sympathetic, however, and do not tell your child that he is not telling the truth or that it is naughty to tell stories. You may be nipping a rising poet or dramatist in the bud! Think how you yourself enjoy embroidering a good yarn and what a bore old Jones is with his literal accounts of his weekend rounds of golf. How you long to stifle him and how you try to do so by burying your nose in the paper. And this reminds me how important it is to be a good listener. There is nothing so deflating to one's ego as a disinterested listener. This is why wives complain so bitterly about their husbands reading the paper at breakfast and not talking to them. What really annoys the wife is that the husband won't *listen*. So try to take an interest in what your youngster is telling you. And as to this question of his telling stories, he really does find it hard to distinguish between what has really happened and what has happened in his imagination. Sally, for example, who at three and a half was much given to wandering both in body and mind, one morning brought me a present of a bunch of red currant blossoms. I knew at once that the bush grew in a neighbor's garden and not ours.

"They're flowers for you," she announced.

"Where did you get them?"

"I have been a long long walk in the country."

"You know I don't like your going on long walks in the country by yourself. You must stay in the garden."

"The fairies tooked me. They say come with me. We look after Sally. The fairies flyed with their long long wings, and the fairies picked the flowers for you and I walk with my long long legs. Then I comed back. It were lovely."

She would often come in from the garden with long excited tales about the wonders she had seen, such as snakes, beetles, lizards and dragons. Heather, now six, disapproved of these dreadful lies and would challenge their veracity. But Sally would never retract a single word and would defend her story even to the point of tears, saying with a crescendo of conviction: "I seed a snake. I seed it. I seed it with my eyes."

Many children have imaginary companions at this age. With Sally it was fairies but it can be another little boy or girl. Besides holding long conversations with these make-believe friends, they are often scapegoats too and are blamed, as Sally's fairies were, for the child's misdeeds. Heather had a friend, half-imp, half-boy, called Jack-the-Jick-Jack. He was often punished harshly and shut up in a cupboard for invented wickedness which she, being a rebellious child, would herself have dearly loved to perpetrate. Sometimes she was Jack-the-Jick-Jack herself. She would answer in his language, which went something like this—"Pom-di-pom-pometty-pom." She talked like this when he did not want to do as Heather was told by her mother, or maybe when she had hit her sister or hidden her toy or broken a cup; it was always Jack-the-Jick-Jack who had been leaping around again and knocked into something.

"Well, you must stop him," I would say irritably. "I never see him but you do, you see him; he's your friend and if he can't behave properly you will have to tell him to go away and live somewhere else. He can't live here."

"Very well, I tell him."

Later she might come back and say, "Jack-the-Jick-Jack says he sorry and he be good now. But I smack him and shut him in the cupboard till he be good. He promise."

And for a little while he would be good, but alas not for long.

Some children at three-plus are extraordinarily verbal and never stop talking. Stern has described the "veritable confabulation mania" of his daughter Hilde. "She often begins sentences without knowing their end. It seems as though the flow of words must not be interrupted at any price, and to avoid any gaps, any sort of padding must be used which, in its turn, becomes the starting point for other associations." Stern also comments upon the interesting association between speech and movement at such times of excessive loquaciousness. The child may hop, tear about, climb up onto a chair and down again, his limbs as active as his tongue, and all combining in an endless flow of movement. No wonder he has earned the name of "little nipper." It is not surprising that

some children suffer if not allowed to exercise speech and movement in this way. If brought up in the cramped living conditions
of one or two rooms for the whole family, they may be retarded
in speech. Inhibition of bodily movements can inhibit speech,
since both are a means of active expression and closely linked
throughout early childhood. It is difficult to allow a child to let

Jack-the-Jick-Jack banished to the cupboard

off steam to his heart's content in an apartment, but get him out
into a recreation ground or a park or on the sidewalk and he will
be able to exercise his body and lungs. His young animal energies
need an outlet.

From this account of the child's verbosity it may be rightly
concluded that his skill in expressing himself has progressed marvelously. Articulation improves with fluency and by three and a
half most of the early mispronunciations are eradicated. Not only
are there no substitutions of one consonant by another, but two

consonants together are often correct, and such difficulties as "spoon," "school," "biscuit," and even "elephant" may be mastered. A lisp, the substitution of "th" for "s," may persist for another year or two, however, as I mentioned earlier. And remember that girls are better at pronunciation throughout than boys and, in fact, boys do not catch up in this respect until six or seven years of age.

Though fluent and articulate, the child of three and a half may still have much to learn with regard to sentence construction and his language may be weird and wonderful at times. When he does not know the correct grammatical construction he improvises, showing real ingenuity in molding language to his own needs. This is real improvisation, not imitation, for he has never heard adults use the constructions he invents.

Valentine gives the delightful example of his daughter at three and a half saying, "You'd never do that, never'd you?" and "Nobody didn't give me no sugar, I'm sour." Sally said once, "I'm busy, I'm the mostest busy." And Heather, reveling in making footsteps in the snow, a joy we can probably all remember, exclaimed, "Listen, my feets doesn't talk!" A little girl pestering her mother for a pony declared, "My bottom's itchin' to get on a horse."

Listening to these variants of our staid and stereotyped adult language shows us the real job the youngster has in mastering language rules. He actually has to talk all the excessive amount he does because this is a necessary language exercise for learning intelligible speech. At two he learns words, nouns and verbs mostly, but this is the first and easiest step in talking, as anyone who has learned a foreign language well knows. It is not enough to know how to pronounce words; one has to learn grammar and the word order of sentences, which make all the difference between sense and nonsense in what you say. So encourage your child in his storytelling and in his strange confabulations by sympathetic listening, interested questions and comments, and lead him to express in words what is going on inside his small head.

Some children are far more verbal than others and, as I have already pointed out, little girls are ever so much better at learning to talk and are far more fluent than little boys; they talk earlier and pronounce words better, an advantage which females have over males in most cases throughout life.

Some very lively and imaginative children and especially small boys have real difficulty in translating into words the images or pictures that float through their minds. When a child has so much to tell you and such limited language at his disposal, his thoughts often run ahead of his speech and he is at a loss for words. Then he may hesitate, repeat a word several times or the first syllable of a word. This is the developmental or physiological stammering, which is a perfectly normal phase in speech development. Most children between three and four years show some characteristics of stammering, but some a lot more than others. It is not stammering, however, and should not be compared in any way to this speech defect. Most parents fortunately never notice this stage of hesitant speech in their offspring, but over-anxious parents may do so and begin to worry unnecessarily. The most important thing is to realize that your child is not stammering and to put this bugbear of a word right out of your head. And for goodness' sake never mention the word "stammering" in front of your child or show the slightest concern. There is really no need to worry and the vast majority of children pass through the phase in a few weeks or months and leave it behind. If you have helped your child in the ways I have suggested in the preceding years he will be well equipped with language and should have no lasting difficulty with speaking.

During the phase of repetition and hesitation, however, there are quite a number of things you can do to help your child. Firstly, review his daily program and ask yourself if he is getting enough rest and sleep. If he is going short, see that he gets more of it. Don't let him get overtired or overexcited and make sure that he follows a sensible and regular routine. Be patient with him but firm. Don't give in once you have said "no," but make sure that you never say "no" unless you really mean it. Don't be afraid of upsetting him by insisting upon obedience. He is far more upset by inconsistent discipline than by strict discipline.

A child needs firm and consistent handling to know how he stands, what he may do or may not do. His security depends on this. He has absolutely no conception of the whys and wherefores of all the dos and don'ts with which parents regulate his life. He conforms to the edicts of father and mother only to please them, knowing that disobedience brings displeasure. You are the lawgivers and he will accept your laws as long as he knows the rules of the game. Don't let young Jim stay up late one night watching television because you are feeling fresh and in a good temper, and then be angry with him when he demands the same treatment the following night when you are feeling jaded and irritable. Father and mother must work out a reasonable plan of dos and don'ts together and then stick to it. Never let young Jim get round one of you and start a rift in the parental ranks. Keep a united front at all times and, if you disagree, argue it out by all means but when the nipper is out of earshot. And another thing while on the important topic of punishment. Don't leave punishment to one or the other parent. This leads to difficulties also. A child will know he can play the mother up who says, "I'll tell your father." Besides having little respect for his mother's authority he will begin to regard his father as an ogre. It is better to give a child a token slap at the time of his offense than to leave punishment till hours later when father comes home.

It is, of course, always better to avoid spanking a child and instead to deprive him of some little treat if he has been really disobedient. But there are circumstances when a toddler is too young to be reasoned with, when the only sensible thing to do is to chastise him. Such circumstances are when a child persists in doing something really dangerous. Heather, at eighteen months for example, persisted morning after morning in trying to grab a shiny silver hot-water jug on the breakfast table. Scolding and persuasion were no good. Eventually I allowed her to touch the very hot jug. It was a sharp lesson but she never touched it or things on the stove again. I am glad I was so ruthless now that I have seen the dreadful scalds and burns on children in plastic surgery wards. At two and a half for no reason at all Heather started a dangerous game of darting off the pavement into the road. Again scolding and warning had not the slightest effect. At last she was almost run over and in the shock of the moment I snatched her back and administered a good spanking. This cured her. Afterward I blamed myself—not for spanking her, but for not doing so earlier. How would I have felt if she had been run over?

After three years old corporal punishment should seldom be necessary and punishment by deprivation quite adequate.

As to the child's hesitant speech, what can you do specifically to help? Firstly, listen to him patiently and let him take his time. Don't hurry him or interrupt his yarn. If his brothers and sisters (assuming he has some) are inclined to interrupt or speak for him, discourage them from doing so.

Secondly, you can help him when he appears to be tied up in knots and cannot get out what he wants to say, not by telling him to speak slowly and not by telling him to say it over again "properly," but by asking him a pertinent question or making an appropriate remark. In this way you can put the words he wants into his mouth. You can clear up his confusion without interrupting him and without directly drawing attention to his speech. He is quite unaware of his repetitions and hesitations probably, so let him remain oblivious of them. When he is launched upon describing a whole exciting incident with so much in his mind that he does not know where to begin or how to proceed, if you ask him a question here and there, it may break the tension and get the words flowing again. If John comes rushing in to tell you that two cars have just driven into each other on the corner and he gets stuck, for instance like this—

"The car ever so fast went wham into the-and-and-the-the-"

This is the moment to put in something like this, since he seems to have forgotten the word other:

"And the *other* car? What happened?"

"It went crash into the other car and they stopped and the-the-man-the-the-car and-and the-"

"The drivers, what did they do?"

"They got out and they shouted—" chuckling.

"And were the cars broken?"

You thus lead him by questions and comments, give him the words he needs and enable him to describe what he has seen.

For a small child to start a real stammer there must be a great deal wrong with him apart from his speech. He must be fundamentally very anxious, and something must be causing this anxiety. For example, I once had a dear little tot of two and a half brought to me because she was stammering so badly. I could scarcely believe that a child so young could stammer until I heard her— then I had to admit Betty certainly was. She would bend right over almost double and go scarlet in the face with the effort to get the words out. Until a few weeks back she had spoken beautifully. Now it transpired that Betty's mother had been much put out when after twenty barren years she learned she was to be blessed with a child. Nevertheless, being a capable woman, she decided to take the disaster sensibly and determined that when Betty arrived she would bring her up very nicely, so nicely that her social life would not really be very much disturbed. She succeeded in producing a model child who could be taken anywhere and relied upon to be seen but not heard. While she enjoyed her bridge parties, little Betty played quietly by herself and all the aunties thought what a wonderful little girl she was.

But quite suddenly things went wrong, to the embarrassment and shame of her mother. Betty's panties were constantly wet and this was a far greater inconvenience tl n her stammer. It was this, in fact, which had driven the mother to seek her doctor's advice, which to her surprise was to take Betty to a speech therapist immediately. Of course the first thing was to teach this mother how to enjoy her little girl and play with her and to adjust her life to the needs of the child. Besides this, Betty needed play therapy, to learn to play as a toddler should. At first she was so pathetically inhibited she could not romp, kick down brick castles, throw sand around, mess or scribble on paper. I shall never forget the day when at last, instead of making little dots on huge sheets of paper, she scribbled vigorously all over them and the table too, and ended by chewing her crayon and spitting it out on her clean white frock. Nor shall I forget her mother's face when she saw the mess! Still, her mother co-operated magnificently and began to think things out for herself. One day she reported that she had been very concerned to discover young Betty in the larder systematically stripping the labels off all the cans. Mother remembered that my instructions were that Betty should not be checked at every turn. Then she had an idea and fetched paper and pencil and scotch tape and as Betty finished with each can mother labeled it.

"You know it wasn't really any trouble and Betty did enjoy herself. It didn't worry me either, her messing up my stores like that. I don't mind her being untidy as I used to, any more."

Needless to say Betty soon stopped wetting her panties and stammering, for now she was no longer anxious and weighed down by the impossible burden of having to behave like an adult to please her parents.

And now, if you are still worried about young Jim's speech, there is just one more thing you can do. Take him to a speech therapist. This specialist can probably put your mind at rest immediately at one interview and, if your Jim needs help, you can be advised what to do. It is always better to consult an expert than lie awake at night worrying. And it is neither foolish nor fussing to seek advice when you feel you are in need of some.

V
Four to Five

A child should always say what's true
And speak when he is spoken to,
And behave mannerly at table;
At least as far as he is able.

                                    R. L. *Stevenson*

The four-year-old is still a baby in many ways but he is growing up fast. The next year sees great advances in development in all directions so that by five infancy is left well behind. Now a responsible, independent and well-socialized little individual emerges ready for kindergarten.

You can see a big advance in intellectual development in your small child's play during this fifth year. He plays more realistically and with less make-believe. In fact he really plays now with a purpose in mind. For example, he announces in advance what he is going to build with bricks and, instead of piling the blocks on top of one another just anyhow, he attempts to construct something which resembles a house, space station or railway, and he may describe what he has in mind as he builds. Bricks may be placed selectively to represent railway lines, bridges and signals. Imagination is vivid enough to invest crude blocks of wood with the necessary symbolism, but imagination requires concrete representation and different constructions are clearly distinguishable. This is a great advance from the play of the toddler content to push a brick around the floor to the accompaniment of appropriate sound effects. There also develops a certain pride in construction and the child is distressed if a game is broken up. It is a good plan therefore to let the young architect or engineer play in some corner where his work can be left for days on end so that he can return and add alterations and finishing touches as he wishes. That a game can hold his interest for days on end is of great importance in character development. It denotes the growth of concentration and ability to stick to a task and to complete it—a developing attitude toward work as distinct from purely frittering time away in aimless play. This is an attitude every child must learn if he is to succeed at school and indeed throughout life.

A child who does not develop such an attitude and flits like a butterfly from one activity to another lacks stability and will find settling down to school work a hard task. This is a real problem in our present age of restlessness and overstimulation, with mechanical aids for amusement. And I mean not only mechanical toys but also television, which creates an appetite for being amused and stifles the ability to amuse oneself. The small child needs to work things out for himself through play devised by himself. He needs to use his hands and his brain and to verbalize to himself as he goes along instead of having all these important educational activities fed to him from a screen.

Playing with other children should be encouraged as much as possible so that your child gets accustomed to children and gets over any shyness he may have with them. Your first efforts at inviting small children in to play may be disastrous, and result in much squabbling with bitter complaints carried back to mother. There is at first very little idea of give-and-take, but this is gradually learned and co-operation with other children slowly develops. Games may still be noisy and boisterous with much tearing about playing Cowboys and Indians. Play with just one other child is easier because communication is easier and real play between children is, as I explained earlier, only really possible when they can talk to each other a little. The four-year-old is capable of becoming deeply attached to another little playmate, who becomes his inseparable companion. I have known children to be heartbroken and upset for months when a friendship like this is suddenly broken up—either by one child moving to another district or being sent to another school.

During this fifth year speech becomes perfect as far as pronunciation goes and few slips of the tongue are now heard. Sentences increase in length, and verbs, prepositions, pronouns and the other more difficult parts of speech are sorted out. Most important of all as an indication of intellectual maturity is the appearance of the causal clause—the use of because or for. "We can't go shopping because it's snowing" reveals the growth of reason, the making of deductions from observed facts. The answers to all these what for, why, how and who questions have enabled the child to appreciate cause and effect and to draw conclusions for himself. This is undoubtedly a great linguistic achievement. With his increased perception and insight the child begins to rationalize and many things hitherto unquestioned now receive mature judgment. This is the reason for many wise pronouncements which are a revelation to the child but amusingly naïve to the adult. "An engine can't talk words." "There aren't real giants." "Rabbits don't drink tea." "It didn't *really* happen," and perhaps a trifle dubiously, "Did it?"

This does not mean though that fairy stories are no longer enjoyed. If anything, they are loved even more intensely since they appeal to the child's sense of fun while he still loves make-believe and magic just as much as formerly. The tigers dressing up one after another in Little Black Sambo's clothes and receiving their just deserts, melting into butter to fry pancakes, which are as brown and yellow as little tigers, is gloriously ridiculous and satisfying while the tale still has the savor of excitement and dangers overcome. The child can identify himself with the trials and tribulations of the little boy and with him emerge triumphant.

The four-year-old's own tales are more literal and less fantastic, though he still embroiders a tale based on real experience and enjoys mixing fact and fiction. But he is well aware he is telling a tall story and I have on occasion played up so well and appeared so gullible that a youngster has taken pity on me and after giving me a serious look he has said, "It didn't really happen, you know. I made that up!" However, not all children are conscience-stricken in this way. The small son of a farmer regularly tried to fool me. Since I was able to make recordings of his conversations with me I can repeat one verbatim. I had told him about a rabbit who visited my vegetable patch and did untold damage, nibbling all the seedlings as soon as they were planted.

"You must find the hole where that rabbit is," he told me. "Then you can put a gun in there and keep it there and he comes out, then shoot him."

"That's a very good idea," I said. "I'm not a good shot like you. I didn't know how I could shoot him running."

"You would do if you got behind a hedge. When you get it sitting down, you can come along and catch hold of its tail."

"Catch it by its tail?"

"It'd bite you."

"Do rabbits bite?"

"Yes, one nearly bit my hand off. Good job it never. I got up and shut it up."

"Was it a wild one?"

"No"—pause—"Yes. John and me went out shooting and I looked under a hedge and I saw two each. Yes, it was sitting in a hole. I had a gun and I poked it out—poked two—in the back. Then they came out on top and it never bit me because I pulled its neck—like that—and killed it dead."

"That was very clever of you."

"You know what they'll do, they'll eat your cabbage up. You ought to put stuff on it—soap. Soap and poison."

"Soap and poison?"

"Soap. You put it up there near where it comes out and put water and soap powder and that would kill it. And some pepper on its tail. And then you let it go and lie down a minute or two, and then it will come out of its hole and then it'll be dead."

I never had a chance of trying this recipe out, however—a fox saved me the trouble!

The child's attempts to explain events give rise at this time to many amusing mistakes, since quite naturally he can only make deductions from his own very limited experience. Jack, aged four and a half, had heard constant references to "electric plant" by his father, who is an electrical engineer. When the family went to spend a holiday in the wilds of Wales in a cottage which only had oil lamps for lighting, Jack asked his mother, "Why doesn't Daddy buy an electric plant?"

"It would be far too expensive," his mother explained.

"But he could get a small one and let it grow."

Of course a child should never be laughed at or made to feel silly when he has committed a howler like this one. He needs a kindly explanation to put him right, and in this case young Jack's father took him along to have a look at a real electric plant!

Motor skill increases enormously in the fifth year too. Our youngster is quick and sure on his feet. He can run fast, wheel round and turn in his tracks while still retaining his balance. He can hop on one leg and go up and down stairs one foot to each step—but still holding the banisters. He can do up buttons, dress himself and attend to his toilet, though corners get overlooked and mother must finish off behind his ears and round the neck, and give his teeth that extra polish. The better linking of eye and hand co-ordination is responsible for better manual dexterity and this becomes more obvious in a child's drawing. At first he could only scribble, then he learned at three years to draw a circle, but between four and five he learns to copy a cross and can draw a man of sorts with a head and limbs, putting in the eyes, nose and mouth, but leaving out the torso. He can color and trace and for this he can hold a pencil or crayon between thumb and forefinger, adultwise, no longer grasping the shaft like a baton. Encourage him to color and draw, trace and cut out, since such activities provide valuable training in visual motor skills. Moreover, the appreciation of shape is valuable preparatory work for learning to read and write. So is work with puzzles—the simple wooden ones which fit into a tray being the most suitable to start on.

This fifth year sees such marvelous advances in performance it is hardly surprising that the child becomes rather conscious of his own brilliance and more than a little too big for his shoes. Although we must commend his achievements and give him his proper due, we must confess that he now passes through a rather obnoxious phase. This is a difficult stage, presenting, in miniature, many of the problems of adolescence. The charming naïveté and modesty of three years old and the anxiety to please are replaced by a conceit and bumptiousness which are well-nigh insufferable at times! This is the stage of showing off. "Look at me," the small boy brags, striking a silly attitude or pretending to fall off his chair. "I'm clever. You can't do that, can you?"

"I shouldn't want to," one may retort coldly.

"No, you couldn't. You're too old and fat!"

Besides conceit he has no sensibility for other people's finer feelings and indulges in outrageous and rude behavior of any and every sort to attract attention. He behaves in a silly fashion in public, no longer shy, but deliberately drawing attention to himself by pulling faces, calling out names, eating noisily and glancing round to make sure he is being noticed. If he can get hold of some bad language he uses it at the most awkward moments, for example, when mother-in-law is visiting. It's no use explaining that you have no idea where he picked up such words; he will probably be glad to enlighten you and further your embarrassment!

He is also adept at storing up the most casual but awkward remarks he has heard in the bosom of the family and reproducing
these for the edification of the very last person one would want
to hear them. You just cannot be too careful what you say in front
of the little horror. My sister, who is given to vivid descriptive
language, once remarked that a dear old friend of the family
kissed like a fish. On this lady's next visit Heather vanished when
she was about to take her leave. "Come along and say good-by
nicely," I instructed her when I found her behind the settee. "I
won't kiss you," Heather announced flatly. "You're a wet, cold
codfish."

It is no good nagging the child as he passes through this phase.
The only thing is to try and understand why he is so insufferable
and treat his misdeeds with tolerance. His behavior is understandable after all. He is no longer me but I, an individual conscious of
his powers to do and say and act independently. It is no wonder
that for a time his new-found power goes to his head. Don't take
too much notice of his going out-of-bounds in this way. Console
yourself with the knowledge that it will pass and he will return to
normal before long. And he does, of course, in due time, never
fear. By five he is once again your own lovable child, and even
more lovable for he acquires a thoughtfulness and consideration
for others which can be quite remarkable. He is sensible and well-
balanced and his understanding of events and of language is such
that you can discuss plans with him, consult him and give him
jobs to do, knowing that he will carry them out responsibly.

The following anecdote demonstrates the maturity of a five-
year-old. Heather was given a watch by her grandmother as a
reward, long-promised, for learning to tell the time. And Sally was
given a pink fluffy rabbit as a consolation prize. Heather, however,
longed for a blue fluffy rabbit with all her heart and secretly she
wasn't at all pleased with her watch. But she was so polite to

her grandmother and thanked her so sincerely, simulating real pleasure over the gift, that I was amazed when she sought me out and said:

"I do want a blue rabbit. If I share my watch with you 'cos you haven't got one and want one *badly*, I could have a blue rabbit and it wouldn't be greedy." (My watch was being repaired at the time.)

I was unable to resist this charming appeal and bought her the coveted rabbit. Heather was absolutely delighted and when I kissed her good night, tucked up in bed with her rabbit, she

Carrying out a responsible job

thanked me again and added, "You can wear my watch, even all the time, but except when we go to see Granny; then I think I'd better wear it, don't you?"

Here we have the not-so-grown-up child with a love of cuddly toys still persisting; the use of reason in getting round the difficulty of having received an expensive present and wanting another; and the social consciousness of appearing "greedy." She is also aware of the possibility of hurting her grandmother and plans how to avoid this. Heather is unable at this age to express fully the reason behind her statements but the insight into the repercussions of her own behavior is clearly there.

What a wonderful development in thought and behavior has taken place in five short years! The teaching of parents during these formative years is all-important and produces these results. But it is no easy collaboration. There is no more difficult job on earth than being good parents. If you can both retain the love and trust of your child and launch a socially responsible individual into the world, you may rest assured you have succeeded. Moreover, if you make a success of parenthood you make a success of life. No matter what other ambitions you fail in, these are unimportant compared to the fulfillment of the task which is yours, when unto you a child is given and you become Mother and Father, dedicated to his upbringing.

Bibliography

Gesell, Arnold, M.D., *The First Five Years of Life*, New York: Harper & Brothers, 1940.

Griffiths, R., *The Abilities of Babies*, New York: McGraw-Hill Book Company, 1954.

Isaacs, Susan, *Intellectual Growth in Young Children*, New York: Humanities Press, 1950.

Keller, Helen, *The Story of My Life*, New York: Doubleday & Company, Inc., 1954.

Lewis, D. M., *Infant Speech*, London: Routledge & Kegan Paul, Ltd., 1951.

Stern, W., *The Psychology of Early Childhood*, London: George Allen & Unwin, Ltd., 1927.

Valentine, C. W., *The Psychology of Early Childhood*, London: Methuen & Company, Ltd., 1942.

Van Riper, Charles, *Teaching Your Child to Talk*, New York: Harper & Brothers, 1950.

Watts, A. F., *The Language and Development of the Child*, London: Harrap & Company, Ltd., 1948.

Table of Important Events in Baby's Life

Name. . . . .   Birthday. . . . .

Age when startled by sudden noise. . . . .

Age when quiets on hearing you talk to him. . . . .

Age when smiles when spoken to. . . . .

Age when coos. . . . .

Age when "talks back" with cooing. . . . .

Age when babbles different syllables. . . . .

Age when sits. . . . .   crawls. . . . .   walks. . . . .

Age when imitates words. . . . .

Words imitated

Age when understands words. . . . .

Words understood.

Age of appearance of first words. . . . .

The first words used

Age when "talks scribble" to himself.........

Age when starts using two- and three-word sentences.........

The sentences he uses

Age when begins to ask, "What's that?".........
Age when begins to ask, "Why, where, how and when?".........
Age when uses "yes".........
Age when uses "I".........

Memorable Conversations 1-2 years

Memorable Conversations 2-3 years

Memorable Conversations 3-4 years

Memorable Conversations 4-5 years